The Creative Brain Guide

The Limitless Potential Within

Kendir Ramiz

The Limitless Potential Within

Introduction: The Discovery of the Creative Brain

Once upon a time, a star was born in the universe, and around this star, a tiny planet began to revolve. It was on this planet that we, complex-thinking, feeling, and dreaming beings, came into existence. Since that day, humanity's greatest quest has been to explore the unknown within. We have asked ourselves: Who are we? Where did we come from? Where are we going? And most importantly, how do we live this life meaningfully and to the fullest? One of the fundamental forces underlying this quest is, without a doubt, creativity.

Creativity is humanity's most unique gift. Without it, nothing would have existed, from the simple drawings on cave walls to the complex vehicles built to explore space, from the profound thoughts of philosophy to the infinite world of art. Creativity is not a talent bestowed only upon artists or inventors; rather, it is a potential that we all carry within us, waiting to be awakened like a seed. Creativity is the ability to see life from a different perspective, to combine what exists in a new way, and to express what is unique to each of us in a singular fashion.

Perhaps you are currently looking at this book with curiosity. I can almost hear you say, "How would creativity benefit me? I am a scientist, an accountant, or a homemaker." But let me assure you of this: as you continue turning these pages, you will see that creativity has a much broader meaning than you think. This book is written to remind you of that inner power, to help you understand how you can unlock it, and to provide you with a tool kit that you can always use. In this journey, I will guide you as both a scientist and a fellow traveler who has personally experienced these explorations, making discoveries in his own depths. What you will find in this book is not just information, but also experience, discovery, awareness, and most importantly, a key to your limitless potential. So, let's embark on this enjoyable journey together.

CHAPTER I:

The Malleable Nature of the Creative Brain – Neuroplasticity, Connections, and Transformation

The Miracle of Neuroplasticity

In one of the most unforgettable moments of my life, I watched a young child successfully catch a ball for the first time. The indescribable joy in their eyes seemed to be a reflection of a newly formed connection in their brain. That day, I once again marveled at humanity's capacity for learning and change. And since then, neuroplasticity has become a phenomenon that has captivated me.

Neuroplasticity, simply put, is the ability of our brain to constantly change and renew itself throughout our lives, just like water can change its shape. Previously, it was thought that the brain remained fixed after a certain age, making new learning difficult. However, modern neuroscience has proven the opposite: our brain, as a result of our experiences and learning, can create new connections at any moment, strengthen existing connections, and even change physically. This is a sign that human potential is limitless and represents a fact that can constantly improve us. Every new piece of information, new skill, or experience opens new neural pathways in our brain. And the more these neural pathways are used, the more powerfully they continue and become permanent. It's just like a path that is constantly used in a forest. While an unused path disappears over time, the paths that are used become permanent.

Let's look at what neuroplasticity means in the context of creativity. This shows us that our creative abilities are not only dependent on our genes or assumptions we bring from birth. On the contrary, it reveals that our brain is suitable for new ideas, approaches, or all kinds of different perspectives. This means that by learning how to nourish the creative spark within each of us, we can create an endless creative universe.

Kendir Ramiz

Neural Pathways and Life Story

Every moment in our brain, every minute of our lives, is like an ink mark drawn on our nervous system. From the first emotional experiences we had in childhood to the complex information we learned in adulthood, each of our experiences creates different and unique roadmaps in our brain. These paths are called neural pathways. And actually, these paths form our life story. Whatever we feel and experience, we transfer them from the abstract side of our mind to the concrete side of our body. For example, a fear, an anxiety, or excitement. The neurons in our body fire. And each time we repeat the emotion, it turns into a permanent and conscious memory.

Every new experience means the birth of a brand new neural pathway. While learning to play an instrument, trying to speak a new language, or interacting with a different culture, connections form between nerve cells in our brain. Just like seeing a new road sign on a path we haven't traveled before, these paths get stronger as they are repeated, become more distinct, and information transfer becomes easier. The more we learn and experience, the more the roadmaps in the brain change and expand. Through neural pathways, we build a flexible brain that is always open to learning and development. Life-long experiences thus take place simultaneously in both the brain and our subconscious.

So, how does this affect our creativity? The mental structuring in our brain gives new meanings to this situation. When we repeat something many times, we not only learn a single subject, but different skills develop in the functioning of the mind, allowing us to have different abilities. Our way of learning also varies according to neural connections. Completely different talents can be acquired by connecting different areas in the mind. We must give ourselves a chance on our own journey for this unique dance of our mind and physical skills.

Kendir Ramiz

Creativity, the Brain, and the Sense of Aesthetics

At one point in my life, I met a street artist. His talent deeply impressed me. They navigate so well between colors and dreams that it seemed as if there was a secret bond between their minds and their brushes. Later, as I watched him, I realized that they were actually beyond the simple people we knew, and I discovered that their neurons worked in such a synchronized way. At that moment, I understood better: creativity is not just about talent, it actually comes with a complex mental symphony! This is how I better understood how unique the brain of a creative person is.

Creative people are those who can use their brains to interpret the world in different ways. Neuroscience shows that in the creative process, many different regions of the brain work synchronously and that the right hemisphere plays an important role in creativity. In the brains of people involved in art, the regions related to visual and spatial abilities become more active and work in stronger communication with each other. The ability to distinguish colors while painting, to create a three-dimensional perception while working with sculpture, and to feel the sense of rhythm while making music occur with the synchronization in our brain. These moments when the sense of aesthetics is born actually reflect the most powerful beats of the symphony that create wonders in the brain.

When we think about what happens in our brain behind creativity, we begin to understand more clearly. A person's aesthetic view comes entirely from the uniqueness of his mind, and in this world where no two people's brains are the same, we are all unique individuals. Thus, art is not just a hobby or skill. On the contrary, it is one of the most powerful reflections of our brain and the most unique expression of our potential.

Kendir Ramiz

Nurturing the Creative Urge

I remember when I was a child, my grandfather would always say to me, "Play is the most important job in the world." That day, I didn't fully understand what he meant. But as I grew older, I better understood that my grandfather's game was actually an exercise for our brains and that it was helpful in directing our thoughts. It turned out that my grandfather was actually training our minds without realizing it. I have seen through my own experiences that a creative brain can be developed through play.

Developing creativity does not just mean waiting for inspiration or having special talents. On the contrary, we can have some secret techniques to activate our brains in different ways. For example, when learning a language or solving a difficult problem, both hemispheres of our brain have to work simultaneously. For this, activities such as mental puzzles, strategy games, and sudoku improve problem-solving skills and stimulate creative thinking. In particular, puzzles and mind games help create new connections in the brain and form a foundation for the creative process. Even walking down a new street or listening to different music in our daily routine relaxes our minds. And it causes different perceptions to arise. We can guess how much our brain will be strengthened with these exercises! That is why, looking at mental exercises as a training program for our minds is the secret key to unlocking our creative potential.

Small Changes for the Creative Brain

I hadn't realized for a long time that there was a connection between the peace and tranquility I felt while wandering in the depths of a quiet forest and creativity. But in fact, I gradually realized that the more peace we find and the more we get rid of stress, the better our brain works. At that moment, I realized that it is not enough to just develop our creative urge; we need to create suitable environments and conditions for it. By making improvements in conditions that do not allow creativity, we aim to keep our minds vigorous and clear.

Thus, everyone who focuses on the creative brain can build a life by making small but effective changes in their lifestyle.

I have seen that creativity also wants to be looked after, just like a good gardener cultivates and feeds the soil. Sleep patterns, balanced nutrition, and the need to exercise are the most important basic needs for a good performance of our brains. Regular sleep ensures that our brain functions work well and also makes it easier to rest. By eating a balanced diet, we provide the energy for our brain and nervous system to work in the best way. In addition, regular physical activity increases blood circulation, thus positively affecting our brain and improving our mental abilities. Staying away from stress is also a good factor. For example, nature walks and open-air meditations help our brain to get rid of unnecessary information and allow us to develop clearer thoughts. Even these small changes can be effective methods to strengthen the creative brain. The creative brain is not just an organ that works on its own, it also interacts with our lifestyle and behavior.

CHAPTER II:

Two Dimensions of the Creative Process – From Inspiration to Concreteness, From Freedom to Discipline

The Neurological Mystery of Inspiration

Remember the first moment an artist touches the canvas. It is as if the brush trembles with his heart and his mind is filled with brand new possibilities at that moment. This feeling is a storm of inspiration. Although these moments always give the same feeling, it is interesting that the mind awakens at different times. Although it sometimes comes suddenly and sometimes slowly to everyone, it is an indescribable emotional experience when the mind is filled with those bright and new ideas. The moment of inspiration is both a fascinating and mysterious experience. Studies in the field of neuroscience show that the moment of inspiration is evaluated as a kind of neurological symphony that occurs as a result of complex processes in our brain. It is necessary to know that it is a neuron dance in the brain where the creative spark suddenly flashes. In this way, we can both concretize the deepest desires of our hearts and create brand new ideas and new emotions. Taking inspiration actually means navigating through the depths of our brain.

So, how exactly does that spark occur in our brain? In fact, moments of inspiration mostly originate from the interaction of different areas in the brain. Thought processes in the brain benefit from deep information in our subconscious. In the moment of inspiration, the default mode network is activated and suddenly emerges, supporting the establishment of surprising connections in the brain. And at the same time, our reward system releases dopamine. It excites us, allowing us to work harder. Although this complex system occurs quickly, it is in perfect coordination. It means that the driving force that activates the creativity that sprouts within us actually occurs through these complex processes. Thus, this magical first spark of the creative process always pushes us to the edge of an unknown.

The Freedom of the Default Mode Network

Imagine you are watching a movie or listening to music. With a moment of distraction, you drift away. At that moment, you are transported to completely different lands. The default mode network (DMN) can be thought of as the place where our mind goes for a walk at such a time. The relationship between creativity and letting the mind flow calmly can actually be understood more easily by looking at the DMN. In other words, when other systems in the brain take a break from their work, a system we call the Default Mode Network (DMN) operates, allowing dreams, ideas, and new possibilities to communicate with different parts of the brain. Thus, by leaving ourselves in this void, we can produce new things. Although it is actually a mind-resting mode, there is also great mobility in the DMN. The deepest depths of the mind are descended into, and by reaching the subconscious that is waiting to be discovered, information that was previously unconnected comes together. Thus, we can be prepared for unexpected surprises.

In neuroscience research, the DMN becomes active when our brain is not dealing with an intense task or when we move away from external stimuli and listen to ourselves. This situation is like wandering freely on a cloud, and when our ideas are released, the chain of thought begins to flow. In this mode, we find time for our previous experiences, future expectations, daydreaming, and even questioning our existence. In this void, we can find ourselves on a new level of creativity with unexpected connections and brand-new perspectives. At that moment, our consciousness seems to open different doors, and reaching new possibilities becomes much easier. One of the most important features of the creative brain is that it gives itself the opportunity to be free, and it is necessary to leave the mind to this journey in the DMN. In this way, we are both open to innovations and the boundaries of our creativity expand.

Transition from Insight to Product

There are times when I go for long walks in my life. At those times, the solution to a problem that I have been struggling with for a long time suddenly comes to my mind. Just like the tiny seeds that emerge on their own in nature germinate, an idea that emerges as insight is ready to germinate in the mind. Of course, in order for a seedling to grow and bear fruit, it must also be regularly nourished and watered. And if we neglect it, unfortunately, we cause it to wither. Insights need to be addressed and nurtured from time to time. This stage also forms the basis of how the first spark will turn into a product after it appears in the mental realm. The more we assimilate and grow it, the more it will appear over time. This stage is the moment when ideas are first assimilated and plans are drawn and put into practice.

In the process of transforming insights into products, the rational thinking center of our brain comes into play and encourages us to progress step by step. The mind starts to build ideas like an engineer, performs the necessary analysis, and continues on its way with planning. The most important thing to do here is to try to preserve the essence of that first moment that came up like a storm in the mind before. The seed of insight is so special that every touch adds value to it. In creative processes, every such new moment will ensure the birth of new ideas and will lead to the formation of a unique dance in the mind.

The Creative Energy of Time

I have been in different environments at very different times. Whenever I wanted to experience that moment of creativity, I always worked at the times that suited me best. One of the most beautiful realities, which perhaps many of us do not know, but which will guide our lives if we know, is that we reach a more creative power as a result of processing time and energy together. The correct determination of timing actually directly affects the quality of the creative process. Within this time, I realized that an excitement of discovery arose from within us. Whenever my brain was at its best, I had a productive and successful day at that time. Refreshing my brain at certain intervals and focusing on the times when I was doing well was turning me into a much more productive person. When I balanced time and energy, I actually reached a more effective creative process.

The energy of our brain varies at different times of the day. For example, according to some studies, while the morning hours are more suitable for analytical thinking, the evening hours lay the groundwork for more intuitive and creative thinking. Based on this information, what we need to do is first realize ourselves and the hours when our body is most active. We need to create a schedule that suits our personal rhythm. For example, we need to keep track of when very good ideas come to our minds. It is also one of the most important to follow when the focus becomes more difficult in creative studies and where that energy drops. And taking a break at that moment helps us both to get more efficiency and to renew our energy level. Thanks to time management skills, we can unlock the creativity within us and get the best efficiency from our energy and creativity.

Confronting Blockages and Moving Forward

No matter how much experience I have, I always get stuck in blockages in the creative process. No matter how many creative people I know, they also face the same problem from time to time. On those days, I would only listen to my inner voice and discover my own self-healing methods. Thanks to my inner voice, I knew that creative blockages are not just a problem. It is actually an indication of a pause or a kind of alarm from the mind. And I know that all kinds of blockages are a good reason for new beginnings. One of the important steps in the creative process is learning to deal with blockages. These challenges also offer opportunities for growth. We must keep in mind that when we manage those moments correctly, we will get to better places.

So, where exactly do creative blockages come from, and what can be done to overcome them? Blockages can arise due to many different reasons: stress, fatigue, lack of self-confidence, anxiety, or perfectionism. Blockages can manifest themselves more with fear and fear of failure. But what you should not forget is that the best way to deal with these difficult processes is to recognize the fear within us. Since we are often our own worst critics, what we need to do is suppress that inner voice and allow the blockages to live their natural process. For example, at a moment when you are blocked, it is important to try to deal with a different creative work, to draw the inspiration fairies to different areas, and to give time to the subconscious. All kinds of blockages can disappear over time, and this process can turn into both a change and a personal development opportunity. Remember that every darkness also contains an enlightenment. It is important to be patient and supportive of ourselves in creative blockages.

CHAPTER III:

Mental Integration and Creative Meditation – Awareness, Freedom, and a Holistic Experience

Open Attention and the Ability to Live in the Moment

When you enter a forest, there are so many different stimuli such as the trees, grass, and bird sounds you see. The attention skill of our brain captures all of these and reveals brand new senses. As our brain perceives all the beauties that our eyes can see, the world begins to gain new meanings. Open attention is not only about focusing on what we see or hear, but also about our mind fully witnessing the stimuli coming from both the outside world and the inside world. It is actually about letting the mind leave itself in an empty space and watching that void slowly fill with new information. These moments, considered together with the concept of awareness, are actually sprouting the seeds of our creativity. When we look at these moments, we begin to witness more how all that stimulus merges with creative inspiration potential and grows.

Open attention represents the ability to keep our mind in the moment, to observe both the external world and the internal world without making judgments, and to embrace experiences in their entirety. It allows us to develop a different perspective and expand the creative wings of our minds. For example, it offers us the power to see a simple object that we see around us in a brand new meaning. Just like it allows us to see even an ordinary stone as a brand new work of art... When we look at it in this sense, it is like proof that there is a spark of creative power in every moment, everywhere, and in everyone. Discovering such creative power will be possible with the expansion of our awareness. Since creativity is actually hidden in the moment, the only thing we need to do to live in the moment is to live our attention with all its openness.

Emotional Freedom and Creative Risk Taking

In some periods of my life, I witnessed that many people were very reluctant to experience some emotions within them. This emotion can be fear, anger, or anxiety. And then I saw that these emotions prevented those people from reaching their potential. For this reason, I understood that it is very important to accept and embrace these feelings rather than shy away from them. Doesn't an artist get inspiration from his emotional world? Emotional freedom is more meaningful in this context, because it makes it easier for us to bring feelings together within ourselves and take creative risks. Thus, when we balance our feelings with our minds, the doors of a creative mind are fully opened. Creativity also expects us to be honest and courageous by simply entering our own world. For this reason, understanding feelings is like an invitation to our own potential and our most creative state.

In our creative process, the guidance of our emotions is of unique importance. Emotional freedom means to embrace each of our emotions without judging, whether positive or negative, to be able to trust our inner voice, and to maintain the curiosity of where that inner voice can lead us. For example, in order to dare ourselves to new and previously unknown paths, we feel compelled to overcome our fear of failure or our anxiety of being liked. Emotional freedom is actually related to our willingness to take risks without leaving the mind under pressure. In order to be able to dare all this, we must first be a companion with our senses. Because there is always an emotion at the center of every creativity. And every emotion of ours is a unique building block of our creativity.

Holistic Awareness, Intuition, and Emotional Depth

I remember the times when I only focused on my mind for a very long time. When I fell into the delusion that I needed to improve my mind, I realized how far I had moved away from the intuitions in my body. Until that day, I realized that I was stuck only in the guidance of the mind until I listened to the voice of my body. Later, I saw that when we build a holistic life in harmony with our intuitions, creativity is also opened up. Creativity is actually revealed when we understand the integrity of the entire universe and create a holistic symphony with our senses. The creative process is related to listening to our intuitions from the depths of our mind, our body, our emotions, and our heart, as well as our mind. As we reach unity, it will reveal its secrets.

Holistic awareness is to direct all our attention not only to our minds, but also to what we feel in our bodies, to the fluctuations of our emotions, and to the intuitions rising from our deepest selves. Just like the inner voice that comes from our heart, our brain provides information flow through intuition and transforms each of our emotions into creativity through the mediation of that information. For example, while dealing with a problem, we may suddenly feel relief in our body. Or while listening to a piece of music, our heartbeats slow down, and we even load new meanings into our emotions. Holistic awareness deepens not only ourselves but also the bond we have with the world. And we understand that we are all a part of that infinite universe. When we manage to be fully synchronized with the universe, we can be more creative, and ultimately, we can build a better life.

Creative Meditation and Invitation to Inspiration

Most people have the following perception about creativity: "It's as if there is a magic formula, and inspiration will explode the moment it knows how to use it." And I always tried this myself. And I experienced in my own journey years later that this was very wrong. Whenever I calmed my mind, new ideas would explode at that moment. Maybe what was always expected of us was not actually to create a formula but to eliminate that mental complexity. This process actually involves opening the door to creativity by leaving the mind in a void. Ever since that day, I have been experiencing the most powerful meditation and creativity by simply letting the mind free. Meditation is a journey of discovery in our inner world, and for this reason, we should look at it as our most natural way, which strengthens our bond with creativity. Whenever the mind relaxes and is free, inspiration is born into us in the most beautiful way.

Creative meditation, unlike the classic meditation practice we know, not only relaxes our minds but also opens an ocean within us for our journey of creativity. In other words, in classical meditation, we exclude the outside and focus only on the inner world, but in creative meditation, we dive more into our inner world, interact with our subconscious, dream of building new worlds, and collect inspiration for ourselves by experiencing deeper experiences. The moment we transform meditation into such a creative ritual, we open those special doors. When we enable the potential for creativity to reach freedom, we can be much more productive and inspiring. One of the most important elements in this journey of creativity is to offer us experiences that will make us who we are and to go on the path of discovering ourselves.

Mental Integration and Small Creative Touches

Do you know that we are all a symbol of creativity? Even on the most ordinary day, we are in a state of being in a creative act. For example, when we choose our clothes, we create a style, when we make coffee, we create our own rituals, and when we make the most accurate sentence to our friend, we do relationship architecture. Like all of these are actually works of art. There is a thought in our minds, and in the small touches we make every day, we reflect it in life. For that reason, we are a whole, and every part of our lives is our unique reflection. The more we integrate mental integration into our lives, the more we will become an ambassador of creativity. We can see the small details that manifest themselves in every area of life as one of the milestones of our creative journey that we will make to ourselves. Living each day with awareness and valuing it is a way to take inspiration every day, and by passing through these doors that open to infinity, we can acquire a more creative identity. Thus, life is not just an experience but also a brand new and enjoyable work of art.

Mental integration is to add a little awareness and a little wisdom to each of our days, and to realize that new potentials are actually hidden in those seemingly ordinary moments. For example, being in the moment while preparing coffee, or noticing details that you have never noticed before while walking on the road, or even writing down every thought that comes to your mind during the day is an invitation to creativity. Such simple but awareness-enhancing moments will one day take us to greater creative discoveries. Thanks to a holistic and integrated creative process, we actually have many ways to transform our own minds and understand the world and all existence. In order to discover the endless creativity lying in our daily lives, we must give a chance to that beautiful start every day. Thus, life transforms into not just an experience, but a brand new and enjoyable work of art.

CHAPTER IV:

Creativity and Brain Connections – Dopamine, DMN, Prefrontal Cortex, and the Evolution of the Brain

The Dopamine System's Journey with Creativity

In some periods of my life, I would feel an indescribable passion for discovery within me. It was as if an invisible hand was constantly pulling me somewhere, filling my mind with new ideas, and pushing me to constantly pursue something new. And at that time, it took me a long time to realize that I was actually under the influence of dopamine, the secret hero of my brain. In my opinion, dopamine is not just a neurochemical, but a magical elixir that fuels the limitless creative fire within us. In other words, a traveler who is always looking for something, novelty, discovery, and trying to find the most original experiences. And let's not forget that dopamine is also a mysterious force that creates new connections in our brains, enables us to learn, and keeps our curiosity alive. And it is the most correct thing to know him on our life journey.

The dopamine system basically regulates our experiences such as learning, motivation, and reward, and in particular, it helps to keep our creative urge active. So, whenever a new idea comes to our mind or when we set a creative goal and start to achieve it, our brain releases a certain amount of dopamine. And as dopamine is released, our level of motivation and excitement increases, thus continuing to support our creative effort. So, in summary, dopamine enables us to seek new and original experiences, thus causing the mind to remain more vibrant and curious every day. For a writer, those brand new lines that he will write, for a painter, to fill the canvas with different colors, or for scientists, the desire to explore a topic they have never known... Actually, all of these are the effects of this magical dance. Let's not forget that when we follow that desire to explore, our creativity continues forever.

The Creative Delight of the Default Mode Network

Although we distill in another realm while the mind is dealing with intense tasks, DMN does not leave us alone at that moment. The default mode network, which we call DMN, always continues to work silently in the background. That day, while my mind was resting, I realized that it was creating a brainstorming on its own. While I continued to daydream, it was as if everything was mixed together. It was as if new connections, different perspectives, and doors to much deeper thoughts were being opened. At that moment, I understood more clearly that the silent architect of my creative processes was the default mode network (DMN).

The DMN emerges when we are not mentally active and usually activates when we focus inward. It enables us to connect with our past experiences and generate new thoughts about the future. It is actually a kind of nest and source of inspiration for creativity. So whenever we move away from the daily hustle, that creative symphony of our brain starts working on its own. It is as if each note has different feelings and meanings, and it unites the universe with melodic harmonies like music in our mind. We should think that we are all the secret heroes of a universal mind network. The DMN makes it easier for us to generate new thoughts the more freedom we give to our minds. In our journey of creative inspiration, we become the magic wand of those moments of free mind. The more effectively the DMN is used, the more creative potential we can have. And we can experience how magical the silence of the mind can be.

The Mastery of the Prefrontal Cortex and Mental Management

There comes a day when we evaluate the ideas that come to our mind. As the magical realm of creativity begins with the initial inspirations, it also needs to be transformed into a concrete form as the final step. It should be thought of as a mental management center.

Whenever I couldn't get out of complex situations or didn't know how to put things together, the prefrontal cortex would activate. In other words, the only part that skillfully managed to guide my mind on the creative journey was the prefrontal cortex.

The prefrontal cortex, or PFC for short, is located at the front of our brain, which manages abilities such as planning, making decisions, staying away from distractions, and solving problems. As we think about our ideas, evaluate them, and try to give them a form, this part of our brain works automatically. For example, it is the most important point in deciding whether the magnificent idea that comes to our mind is realistic or not. At the same time, all responsibility belongs to this area for us to proceed step by step in a planned way. In short, we see that the creative journey is not only about dreaming, but also about putting those dreams into practice step by step. For this reason, it is important to both free our imagination and keep our rational management power in balance. Thanks to the PFC, we can both provide a harmonious transition to both worlds and keep our minds under control.

Kendir Ramiz

The Harmonious Unity of the Brain's Creative Networks

I am always fascinated by the perfect balance and harmony of nature. It is as if all the elements of the universe create a common symphony. In the same way, different parts in our mind come together and perform a perfect dance with a unique rhythm. When I had the opportunity to see the mind moving in harmony at that moment, I realized how dependent they were on each other. I saw how each region of our brain offered a creative power as a whole and witnessed how it worked in a synchronized way.

The brain cannot work alone; Our brain is both a large network consisting of different parts in terms of creativity and a marvel of collaboration. To come up with an idea or to get inspiration at that moment, the mind works in harmony with all regions of the brain, not just one region. And all those regions become harmonious with each other at every step of the ideas. And in this system, the dopamine system, DMN, and PFC also cooperate for their own roles. It establishes connections with emotional regions, and as a result of all this harmony, each of our ideas begins to gain completely different meanings. It is as if the mysterious rhythms of our brain guide this magical and harmonious dance of creativity. As we dive into ourselves, our mind becomes free on the way to meet infinite possibilities with this cooperation, and our creativity tries to reach its peak.

The Evolutionary Journey of the Brain and Creativity

Like most people, I sometimes marvel when I look at our species, humanity, and the potential of our brain. And I think, where did this story of creativity begin? How did we get from the Stone Age to space travel? Looking at neuroscience, I see that what we call the mind has transformed into a completely different potential as a result of millions of years of evolution. If we look at the history of humanity, it is quite possible for us to see how powerful creativity is in developing and transforming our brains. In other words, an evolutionary journey of the human species from the past to the present allows us to see both how it shaped our creative power and how it transformed it in us.

Throughout that evolutionary process, the growth of the human brain not only enabled the mind to think but also to open new avenues. While creativity existed initially to solve problems, it later took on a very effective role in organizing our social life. They have been inventors in the fields of art and technology, and have transformed our lives for the better each time. Our capacity to learn and adapt enables us to develop a new structural feature in our brain, and the synapses in our brain gradually increase. And we have reached the perfect human consciousness and unlimited creative ability that we are experiencing now. Even after all these mentioned, the evolutionary journey is not over; the importance of creativity brings together the answers to all the questions in our lives. For this reason, when we realize our creative power, we see that we can build a new and unique future in harmony with our brain.

CHAPTER V:
Practical Creativity Development Techniques: C.R.E.A.T.E., Flow, Incubation, and Insight

C.R.E.A.T.E. Technique and Step-by-Step Creative Journey

I have always faced the question in my life, "How can creativity be learned or developed?" Of course, this was not such an easy question, but then I developed a special compass for creativity within myself, and I understood that it was as easy as taking a step with it. I realized that this compass wasn't just about inspiration, but a structured way to bring creative ideas to life. This led me to develop what I now call the **C.R.E.A.T.E.** technique, and it has allowed me to experience creativity in all its aspects step by step. It's like I discovered that every creative endeavor has its own map, and my map is the **C.R.E.A.T.E.** compass.

Creativity can be seen as a journey with this compass. If you are ready for an adventure journey full of new and unusual things, let's begin!

C.R.E.A.T.E., an effective method of developing creativity step by step, consists of 6 separate stages and becomes a companion for us in all our creative processes: **"Curiosity, Reflect, Explore, Articulate, Transform, Evaluate"**.

The **"Curiosity"** stage is the very first step, where we embrace our innate sense of wonder and openness to new ideas. It's about approaching the world with a beginner's mind, like a traveler exploring uncharted territory, always asking "what if" and never losing that sense of discovery.

In the **"Reflect"** stage, we shift our focus inward. We take the time to contemplate, not just observe, allowing our minds to delve into the details of our surroundings and our own thoughts. It's about deepening our awareness by pausing and truly feeling, sensing, and thinking about the world around and within us.

The "**Explore**" stage is when we let go and allow our subconscious to delve into the depths of our minds, our own internal mental sea. We are free to consider connections between ideas that initially seem unrelated, allowing our minds to make new pathways. We explore possibilities without judgment.

Then, having let the seeds of our ideas germinate in the previous stages, in the **"Articulate"** stage, we take these initial concepts and begin to give them form and substance. This is when our creativity takes a more tangible shape, and we communicate our vision to others, allowing our ideas to leave our minds.

Next, in the **"Transform"** stage, we take the articulated ideas and mold them further, shaping them through our creative actions. This might involve rewriting a draft, revising a design, adding a new melody, and letting it evolve and transform into its true potential.

Finally, in the **"Evaluate"** stage, we step back with an objective eye, and we analyze the resulting product of our creative process. We scrutinize it, acknowledging its strengths and weaknesses. This critical analysis allows us to learn, improve, and continue to grow with every creative endeavor. In short, **C.R.E.A.T.E.** is that reliable guide that is with you throughout your creative journey, from that first spark of curiosity to the final evaluation and improvement.

Flow State and Losing Yourself in Creativity

At a certain time in my life, there were moments when I was doing what I enjoyed and I got lost in that job. In those moments, it was as if the world stopped for me and I would only focus on that moment. All my senses were engaged in a harmonious dance, and everything around me had disappeared. In other words, I had witnessed a magical flow moment. At that time, I learned the name of that special state where we reach the peak in creativity; Flow! Being in a state of flow helps to free the mind and to explore creativity in all its aspects. In other words, we reveal our unlimited potential by completely letting ourselves go into the flow at the moment when we enjoy doing it. This gives us endless satisfaction. And this satisfaction is one of the most powerful feelings we will reach in creativity.

The flow state is basically a state of mind where we completely dedicate ourselves to the work we are doing and reach the peak of focus. At that moment, we move away from the concept of time and space and get fully immersed in that moment. In fact, you become one with the work you are doing and you reach a complete feeling of satisfaction by forgetting what you are doing. That experience is completely unique to you, and that moment is the most effective time for what you are dealing with. We can make the best use of that moment, and what we need to do is to be able to focus on our

Incubation Period and the Maturation Process of an Idea

At one point in my life, I had tried for months to find the answer to a question that I was constantly concerned about, but then I gave up and decided to just free my brain. One morning I woke up and, without thinking, an insight appeared in my mind. It was as if the question in my mind had been solved by my subconscious during that incubation period. At that moment, I was amazed by the silent but equally effective power of the "Incubation Period" in the creative process. In other words, I had learned that our subconscious was at least as talented as we were. Sometimes it is necessary to take a step back and both move away from that complexity and leave ourselves in a void.

The incubation period is actually the quiet time when we put creative problems aside and push our subconscious to find solutions related to that subject. When we work on a project for a long time and cannot reach a conclusion, we consciously stop working and give our minds a break. However, at the subconscious level, data related to that project actually continues to be stored, and each of them opens doors to new creative universes by transforming into brand new ideas. During this process, we can relax our minds by engaging in activities such as walks, music, and enjoyable reading moments, and thus leave ourselves in a void. Although the incubation process seems silent from the outside, it is the most special part of a kind of creative transformation process within us, and thus new discoveries become much easier when we give our brain the necessary time and chance.

Moments of Insight and the Surprises of the Mind

There are unexpected moments in life. For example, you solve a problem that you have been thinking about for a long time while doing nothing, and even an inner voice may suddenly appear in your heart. Actually, all of these are the very essence of the enlightenment called "insight." This event was one of the most beautiful surprises of my life. The answer I was waiting for suddenly appeared in my mind as a result of an inner journey, and I realized at that moment that the mind was doing some magic on its own. Thus, I understood how important the concept of insight was and that it was a discovery that suddenly appeared in our brain. In other words, each insight is like a momentary enlightenment in our brain. And remember that the spark of this enlightenment also leads our creativity to shine in a unique way.

Moments of insight are when we understand the sudden solution of a new problem or situation that was not previously in our minds and an awareness of a sudden realization appears. In other words, the mind is a journey to a moment where we comprehend the complex in a very simple way. Something that we could not fully solve no matter what we did until that moment can reach a solution with that spark and suddenly turn into a new invention or a brand new work. Insight should not only be evaluated as a gift created by our brain on its own, but also as an invitation for us to discover the magic of that mind. We can and expect that invitation every moment. And it should be known that insight is always ready to come.

The Constructive Power of Criticism in the Creative Process

It had taken me time to realize that my creative process was a long journey. Eventually, I discovered that I was not alone. I learned that when the ideas growing in my mind entered the world of other people, I needed to understand how they appeared, and then I learned. I learned that there were different people who evaluated what I did and that they were as involved in the work as I was. So, we are not completely independent of a work when we do it anymore. It was at that moment that I saw that we needed to look at our own work with an outside eye and that we needed a new window. Criticism is like looking in a mirror during our journey. Taking the perspective of someone else while showing what we have done actually always makes very valuable contributions to learning and developing ourselves.

Feedback always has a very important place in the creative process. Because when we receive criticism, we always get the opportunity to question our own perspective, and through this, we learn a lot from our mistakes. Of course, we hear different comments because everyone's thoughts are different. And that is exactly when we need to create a roadmap for ourselves from these criticisms. And what we need to do is to see this process as a personal development opportunity, to learn, and to be open to development. Especially by experiencing all kinds of feedback in order to develop ourselves and new creative experiences in different ways, we should enrich this journey each time. In fact, thanks to this, our creative process takes on a whole new meaning by feeding on constructive criticism. Thus, with every touch on our work, we add more value to ourselves. Remember that criticism is always a path to improvement and excellence.

CHAPTER VI:
Creative Wisdom – Discovery, Evaluation, Application, and Creativity as a Whole

The First Step of the Discovery System in Creativity and the Search for Meaning

I have always lived my life as a student curious about new discoveries. My curiosity has always been a guiding light for me. Of course, in all this journey, I realized that our ability to be curious actually resembles an inner compass. Our desire to discover has always risen from within us towards the unknown. What I had experienced until that day was always full of curiosity, and the desire to know and understand formed the flow of my entire life. And I have always noticed until that day that we are fed by the unstoppable power of the desire to learn. That is why curiosity is the first step in our journey of creative wisdom. Whenever you are looking for a beginning, let your compass always be made of curiosity.

The discovery system is known as the beginning of our concept of creative wisdom. We can encounter a subject that arouses curiosity and interest within us at any moment, and we should always see this as a call to the unknown and listen to this call. While we research those things we do not know, we should also pay attention to being open to new experiences. When we become curious about new fields, our inner world turns into a state full of completely different emotions. This system not only helps to generate ideas but also helps in addressing different issues such as problem-solving. In fact, in creativity, we should always be like curious students who are eager to learn and be willing to discover everything living and inanimate around us. By realizing that there are innovations and unique opportunities at every moment and everywhere, we should continue our way confidently towards our next creative experiences. Curiosity is always the best companion that guides our creativity.

The Place of the Evaluation System in Creative Thought and the Power of Analysis

The creative process is actually like a puzzle consisting of many different parts, and each stage is important. Let's talk about one stage, while taking those first steps, excitement arises within us with enthusiasm. What we need to know then is that all emotions are valuable, but we need to keep reason and logic in balance and test every idea we find. In that process, my critical side always continues to be active, and thus, I always reach creativity by creating a solid foundation for my ideas. For this reason, in a creative wisdom, it is necessary that every idea is suitable for both the mind and the heart, without just being caught up in the excitement of the first step.

The evaluation system provides a critical perspective to assess the soundness and how good an idea is each time we generate a new idea. In fact, it is a way of creative wisdom to produce new things and to know the value of what is produced. When we scrutinize all that we have produced, find the missing points or weak sides in them, and make the necessary contribution to them, we get one step closer to perfection. Our analysis skill is very important at that evaluation moment, and it makes it easier for us to understand our own potential and strength. In other words, evaluation is always active as a kind of analysis tool in the creative thinking universe of our mind. For this reason, we must continue our journey of creativity and knowledge with a critical awareness, and we must also know that knowledge can provide us with a power. When we address creativity together with wisdom, we develop ourselves more through new experiences and awareness.

Application System and the Transformation of Ideas into Reality

A creative person is not just someone with ideas and dreams, but also a person who can make those dreams come true. For many years, I have studied people who have been trying to bring together many creative ideas and create brand new works. As a result of all those studies, I learned that the ability to apply is as valuable as inspiration, and the important first step is to bring that dream into a concrete form and turn it into reality. And I understood that it is necessary to implement those valuable ideas in order to bring them to life, otherwise, unfortunately, the value of those ideas would not be known. At that moment, I realized that we were stepping towards creative wisdom, that is, we had learned that we could put the world into a kind of influence mechanism with our mental ability. Therefore, all that remains to be done is to enjoy life with the potential we have.

The application system is the reflection of creativity in the real world, not in the realm of imagination. There are missing aspects even in your best ideas, but what is important is to ensure their completion. We must unleash all the power in our creative potential and be able to mature our ideas and continue on our way by using all our skills. Here we must activate our application skills, criticism, determination, and discipline. By turning these ideas into reality, we not only reach personal satisfaction, but also add meaning and begin to transform everything from scratch. So, as can be seen, the application system is a system that values the creative process not only as the beginning but also to the end to the same degree. And it adds value to its value with the fact that each application can be a creative work.

Development Stages of Creative Wisdom and the Maturation Process

I realized how special the mind is in this process, how differently it thinks, how much it can discover its creativity... As I lived, I came to have greater meanings not only with my own individual world but also with all kinds of experiences that developed around me. Creative Wisdom was like that, bringing with it development in the mental process that continued to reach towards that unlimited freedom that came from within. I realized how beautiful wisdom was... As much as it offers balance in life, it transformed and beautified my creative processes that much. Because, as in the entire universe, every piece of knowledge gave birth to new knowledge, and new inspiration gave birth to more new production. With all of this, wisdom actually leads us to create a complete harmony and balance. For that reason, while we learn, we grow, while we grow, we mature, and we must accept that every journey takes us to brand new lands.

Creative wisdom is not gained in an instant. It only requires a process, and it deepens with continuous development, and it deeply experiences that maturation journey in each stage. Every new experience helps us and acts as a compass on that path. In the first stage, the sense of curiosity and discovery is dominant, and we gain experience. Later, we take into account the entire critical evaluation system, and as we see our mistakes, we ask ourselves questions and show development, and then as the last stage, we make what we have achieved better and share it with everyone, creating an exchange of information. The more we learn, we add much more to that maturation journey, and we now make sense of creativity with our own experiences and knowledge. In fact, all wisdom in the universe passes through experiences and maturity, and thus it transforms into a deeper and more unique state. Creativity is so effective on the path to wisdom that it completes that cycle that lasts forever.

The Key to a Meaningful Life with Awareness

A creative life is actually a whole. It is not only limited to creating a work or taking inspiration and writing, I have always wanted that wisdom to touch all the moments of my life. Until that day, I understood that when we started to integrate creativity into all kinds of different areas, that is, when we fully internalized it, it had a much greater meaning. Whatever I learned, I always wanted to transfer it to my daily life, and thus even my moments that seemed ordinary turned into creative adventures. For example, when I encountered a problem, instead of addressing it immediately, I would address those problems differently by internalizing all kinds of creative processes and finding completely new and unexpected solutions. And again, I know that if we make room for that knowledge in our lives in some way, we can both make our lives meaningful and continue our lives with that inspiration by turning inward.

Applying creative wisdom in our daily lives is very easy, and the important thing is to always look at this event with a creative eye. First of all, we need to let ourselves realize everything in the first stage, and then we need to be open to learning at any moment and deepen with every piece of information. We should attach importance to criticisms; all criticisms, positive or negative, are part of our development. We must draw brand new lessons from mistakes every time, so it becomes much easier to implement new applications. When we follow our own development and focus on our talents, sharing this cycle with other people from time to time in order to support them will keep that endless creativity cycle alive throughout our lives.

CHAPTER VII:

Unlocking Creative Potential – Routines, Environments, Exercises, and an Endless Journey

Creating Daily Routines and Developing Creative Habits

In my long journey, I experienced that creativity is not a secret but a way of life. Rather, I realized that instead of constantly waiting for that inspiration, we needed to constantly nourish it in our lives every day. I said to myself that when I organized each day with my different rituals, I was able to protect my energy and create my own unique life. Although there are many people who define routines as boring, they are a combination of discipline, peace, and productivity, and even a kind of seed of permanent creativity. If we want our creative energy to never run out, we must create a regular routine, and thus, by being more ready for inspiration at any moment, we can take a step on the journey of brand new discoveries. Those routines always hold our hands in that creative process and provide us with both a source of inspiration and motivation. So, if we want to live a creative life, we can create small moments that we can repeat regularly.

Daily creativity routines allow us to keep our creative minds alive and ready, just like a musician plays his instrument every day. A creative routine is actually about dedicating ourselves to our own originality by placing activities in our day that will feed our minds in different ways. For example, it may be an ideal start for a writer to take notes and write every morning, for a painter to delve into different color tones and look for inspiration, and for a scientist to access new resources and improve himself. Later, we can do this by thinking about our daily life and setting aside time for ourselves or developing new hobbies. Every minute devoted to creativity is a unique opportunity for mental development, and over time, those patterns break, and our creative routines become more fluid. The only thing that needs to be done to take a step towards creativity is to open our day to a new adventure. Actually, there is endless creativity hidden in our lives that we are not always aware of, and we can create a tiny routine for every day in order to reach it. Thus, we both keep our door of inspiration open at all times and see that our greatest supporter is our minds.

Designing Creative Environments and Transforming the Spirit of the Space into Creativity

It wasn't difficult for me to understand how much the places I saw affected both our mood and our sources of inspiration. Actually, every place carries traces of the emotional depth and inner state of the people it reflects, and those who are ready to be aware of those moments and be affected by them can capture those inspirations. For example, I have always been very impressed by the magic of nature; I have always set the calm atmosphere of nature as a guide for myself. What we call a place is not so simple; every detail actually has a very important meaning and emotion. A creativity space created with awareness will always have an inspiring and supportive effect. The important thing is to transform it into a place where we will feel both physically and mentally at home and where we will be completely liberated. Every place is a part of brand new and unexplored infinite universes, and we can only address it freely.

We should transform creative environments not only within physical boundaries but also into an inner world. Inspiration cannot be created in a place by simply adding empty walls or furniture; what is important is to find all the elements that can nourish creativity with all our soul and emotion. It is much easier to find new and more original ideas in areas where we feel comfortable and safe, and it should not be forgotten that that special place is the place where our creativity is reflected. That is, every place where we can include creativity, from the smallest arrangement on our work table to the finest detail of the street we walk on, is our place. With our slightest touches, we build an inspiring space suitable for us, and we only reflect our creativity to the outside world. A place we call a creative space is a source of personal expression, peace, and motivation in its entirety. Therefore, every place we are in should always take both our hearts and our minds on an adventure. Thus, we can draw new paths to a world full of inspiration.

Nurturing Creative Thought with Mental Exercises and Keeping the Mind Active

While trying to explore the mysteries of the brain in more depth, I realized that it could be developed like a muscle every day. Even though the mind was busy with exercises, it could travel to different dimensions. Just like an athlete who exercises constantly gets better results. I witnessed moments when our brain wanted to learn more and improve itself a little more every day, and I know that every mental exercise offers completely different possibilities to the brain. The more we take care of our minds, the more we could understand how flexible the limits of our creative potential could be. I understood that as much as we strengthen our brain, we are actually giving great support to our creativity. That is why it is always important to exercise our mental muscles while exploring creativity, and it helps us learn that creativity is not just a talent.

It is important for us to keep our creativity muscles active at all times through mental exercises. To give examples of these, we can include different mind games such as puzzles that we can push the limits of our minds every day, or we can keep our subconscious active by writing down the words and thoughts that come to our mind at once. We must try different ways of thinking and address the world from different perspectives at all times, and we must also occasionally give up our routine behaviors. Dreaming more, writing, and putting forward brand-new ideas leads us step by step on that exciting journey to creativity. Let's not forget that all these mental journeys and training will not only allow us to be creative, but also to overcome all kinds of difficulties in our lives more easily, and we must continue to strengthen the foundations of our creativity. For this reason, let's try to keep those muscles alive by keeping them active and dynamic at all times!

Kendir Ramiz

Developing and Interacting with Relationships and Creative Communities

I learned something very important in life; no one could live alone like an island, and that's why one day I decided to join a community to listen to new ideas with my own ideas. I later discovered that embracing not only individual but also common and brand new experiences had an impact on how much it helped me develop a brand new creative perspective. Everyone was actually transforming that common ground with their ideas, creating new sources of inspiration. Thus, I understood that we can both develop ourselves and increase our inspiration each time, not only alone but also together, and this is the power of unity. In that common interaction, it is not only about sharing our knowledge but also about exchanging a kind of emotion and being able to understand each other at a common point.

One of the basic building blocks of creativity is actually through correct relationships and creating a common pool of ideas with a creative community. When those ideas are reflected and find support, they can bring new perspectives and take us to a completely different world. And every idea is actually a brand new seed. A new source of inspiration can be created for everyone at that moment, and we can find ourselves in brand new creativity projects. When we interact with creative communities, we also expand the ways of discovering new learning each time, and we now know that those ideas not only pave the way for ourselves, but also hold a very beautiful mirror to those relationships. Now, we are discovering new meanings by embracing our creativity together, not alone, but by creating common mental universes, and we know that no creator is alone. In other words, we must be more nourished by the awareness of being able to create inspiration not only in ourselves, but also outside with that togetherness. And every creative unity is actually the most correct step taken for us to transform both ourselves and the world anew.

Kendir Ramiz

The Contributions of Creativity to Life, Its Universal Power, and Its Unlimited Possibilities

When I look back on my life, I see how creativity can be a transformative force against life, and I see that creativity is never limited to a certain moment or period; on the contrary, it offers a hidden and unlimited energy in all kinds of experiences. The most important thing I realized was that with everything I added to my life, creativity was not just a talent, but also about embracing that life and being able to bring a completely different perspective to it. And the more willing we are to embrace that creativity, the more we embark on a journey to new lands in our minds, and we take exciting steps towards the mysterious depths of ourselves. We understand that all the limits are just lies created by our minds, and once we turn to our hearts again, we can see that there are more different possibilities, and we can build brand new worlds with the unlimited power of creativity.

With our creativity, we shape our lives in a way and create a unique journey where we deeply feel its meaning. And thus, finding new solutions, looking at problems from a completely different perspective, breaking those boundaries, and giving new forms to our lives. With this unlimited potential, we both bring a new enlightenment to societies, open different dimensions to science and technology, and carry the richness of art and culture to completely different lands. In short, in this journey of infinity, what we need to do is to always believe in ourselves, our hearts, and our inspiration, and our greatest awareness is to be aware that with every creative step, we are opening new worlds both within and outside us. In each of our experiences, creativity is an inexhaustible energy, and thus every possibility changes and transforms this world, and once again we say that creativity is an unlimited potential within us and each of us seems to have come into the world to fully reveal it. So, align with the universe, feel it, and at that very moment, let inspiration live in you, and know that creativity is your most ancient gift.

Epilogue:

The Voice of the Light Within and the Limitless Potential Waiting to be Discovered

Yes, my dear fellow traveler; as we come to the end of this long-term adventure, let's always remember this. All this journey was actually to find, discover, and nourish the creative spark in each of us. Let's not forget that we all had many jewels waiting to be awakened within us, brand new worlds waiting to be discovered, and a limitless creative potential waiting to shine. Now we know all those secrets, and we continue to meet ourselves in a more different way. We see that creativity was a lifelong journey that should be addressed as an experience, contrary to certain patterns and limits. Everything we learned throughout the journey and our own experiences became even more meaningful and helped us access that magical power within us.

Creativity is like a star that is constantly waiting to shine within us, and if we nurture it, it will always light our way. The most important thing I want you to keep in mind from this book is that creativity is an innate feature that exists in every human being. We can both add new perspectives to life and strengthen it every time by simply transferring it to our small lives. After this adventure, we are much more aware of ourselves and the infinite power of our brains. As we continue our next adventures, let's always keep our own unique potential and talents in mind. Let's remember that nothing in the universe is constant, and as we change, we are transforming the world. And if we are full of new dreams and believe in the limitlessness of what we can do; we must continue on new paths. Let's not forget that this creative journey is not over; on the contrary, it is evolving into a more powerful and meaningful journey in each of our new moments. Let's hold on tightly to the creativity within us and continue to shine it no matter the cost.

www.ingramcontent.com/pod-product-compliance
Lightning Source LLC
Chambersburg PA
CBHW051844250726
48659CB00005B/2014